Machines in the Home

USING SIMPLE MACHINES

Caroline Snow

PICTURE CREDITS
Cover: man preparing food in kitchen © Ron Chapple/Taxi/Getty
Images; Caroline Hyde-Brown embroidering with sewing machine
© Jacqui Hurst/Corbis/Tranz; boy eating at dinner table © Tom
Stewart/Corbis/Tranz.

page 1 © Andrew Brookes/Corbis/Tranz; page 4 (bottom left),
Corbis; page 4 (bottom right), Photodisc; page 5 (top) © Patrik
Giardino/Corbis/Tranz; page 5 (bottom left) © Corbis/
Tranz; page 5 (bottom right), Corbis; page 6 © Norbert Schaefer/
Corbis/Tranz; page 7 (left) © Bettmann/Corbis/Tranz; page 7
(right) © Greg Brookes; page 8 (top left), Photodisc; page 8 (top
right) © Scott Roper/Corbis/Tranz; page 8 (bottom), Photodisc;
page 9 © Ariel Skelley/Corbis/Tranz; page 10 © Raymond
Gehman/Corbis/Tranz; page 11, Corbis; pages 12–16
© Macmillan Publishers New Zealand; page 21, Corbis;
page 29, Corbis.

Illustrations: pages 10–15, 17–18 by Andrew Aguilar;
pages 23–26 by Pat Kermode.

Produced through the worldwide resources of the National
Geographic Society, John M. Fahey, Jr., President and Chief
Executive Officer; Gilbert M. Grosvenor, Chairman of the Board;
Nina D. Hoffman, Executive Vice President and President, Books
and Education Publishing Group.

PREPARED BY NATIONAL GEOGRAPHIC SCHOOL PUBLISHING
Ericka Markman, Senior Vice President and President, Children's
Books and Education Publishing Group; Steve Mico, Vice President
and Editorial Director; Marianne Hiland, Executive Editor; Richard
Easby, Editorial Manager; Jim Hiscott, Design Manager; Kristin
Hanneman, Illustrations Manager; Matt Wascavage, Manager of
Publishing Services; Sean Philpotts, Production Manager.

EDITORIAL MANAGEMENT
Morrison BookWorks, LLC

PROGRAM CONSULTANTS
Dr. Shirley V. Dickson, Program Director, Literacy, Education
Commission of the States; James A. Shymansky, E. Desmond Lee
Professor of Science Education, University of Missouri-St. Louis.

National Geographic Theme Sets program developed by Macmillan
Education Australia, Pty Limited.

Published by the National Geographic Society
1145 17th Street, N.W.
Washington, D.C. 20036-4688

ISBN: 978-0-7922-4754-8
ISBN: 0-7922-4754-X

Product 41994

Printed in Hong Kong.

2008 2007 2006
3 4 5 6 7 8 9 10 11 12 13 14 15

Contents

Using Simple Machines

When you hear the word *machine*, what is the first thing that comes to your mind? Perhaps you think of a dishwasher or a vacuum cleaner. These are both machines, but a broom and a knife are also machines. Basically, a machine is any kind of device that helps you do something more easily. People use simple machines every day—at home, in sports, on construction sites, and in health care.

 ## Key Concepts ....

1. Machines use force to help people do work.
2. There are six simple machines.
3. Compound machines use two or more simple machines operating together.

Where Machines Are Found

In the Home

Simple machines help people with many different tasks in the home.

In Sports

Simple machines are a part of many types of sports equipment.

In this book you will learn about simple machines used in the home, such as this knife.

In Construction

Simple machines make the construction of buildings possible.

In Health

Simple machines are an important part of health care.

Machines
in the Home

Look around your home. What machines do you see? A vacuum cleaner is a machine found in a home, and so is a coffeemaker. But what about a knife or a pair of scissors? These things are also machines found in the home.

Some machines in homes have moving parts, and some do not. Some machines run on electricity, and some do not. All these machines do one thing, though. They make jobs around the home easier.

> A vacuum cleaner is a machine with many moving parts.

Machines – Past and Present

There are many machines in people's homes. Some of these machines are based on tools from long ago. Long ago, people used sharp rocks for cutting and chopping their food. Today, they use knives, which are modern machines with sharp edges.

People once used very basic tools to prepare and cook food.

Today, we use many tools to make cooking easier.

Force and Work

To understand how machines operate, you need to understand **force** and work. Force is something that makes an object move, stop, or change. When you push open a door or stop it from slamming shut, you use force. When you roll out pizza dough, you use force.

force
something that moves, changes, or stops an object

Force can make an object move.

Force can stop an object's movement.

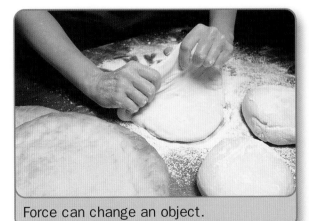

Force can change an object.

In science, **work** is done anytime a force moves, stops, or changes an object. For example, you are doing work when you eat your food. The force of your chewing changes the food so you can swallow it.

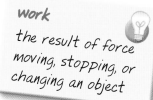

work
the result of force moving, stopping, or changing an object

Much of the work that people do is not easy. Some work requires a great amount of force. People cannot do this work just with their bodies. So they invent **machines** to help them.

machines
tools or other devices that help people do work

The family is doing work while eating. Can you explain why this is so from a scientific point of view?

The Six Simple Machines

There are six **simple machines**. Simple machines are designed to change how forces act.

simple machines
devices that change
how forces act

The Wedge

A **wedge** is an object with one or more sloping sides. The wedge may end in a sharp edge or point. People use wedges to cut or split things. An ax is a type of wedge. You use the sharp edge of an ax to cut into wood. The sloping sides of the ax split the wood apart.

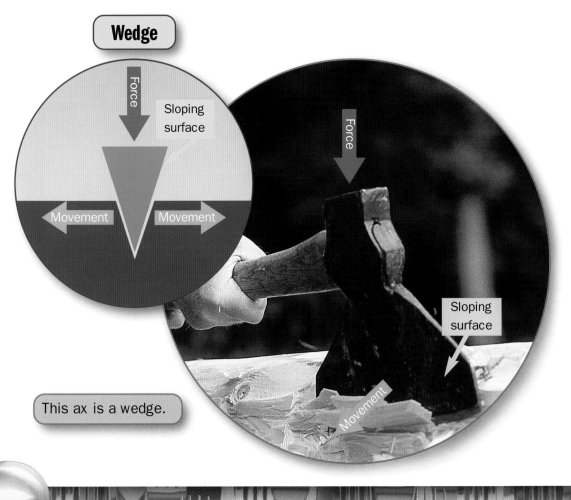

Wedge

Force

Sloping surface

Movement   Movement

Force

Sloping surface

Movement

This ax is a wedge.

The Lever

A **lever** is a straight bar or rod. A lever turns or rotates on a fixed point called a **fulcrum**. By using force on one part of a lever, people can move something that is attached to another part of the lever. The thing the lever moves is called a **load**. A lever can be used to reduce the force needed to move the load.

Lever

Load

Bar

Force

Movement

Fulcrum

This seesaw is a lever.

Load

Movement

Bar

Force

Fulcrum

The Inclined Plane

An **inclined plane** is a flat, slanting surface with a high end and a low end. A ramp is an example of an inclined plane. People use inclined planes to move loads up and down. It takes less force to push loads up an inclined plane than to lift them straight up.

This entrance has a ramp.
A ramp is a type of inclined plane.

Inclined Plane

High end

Low end

Force

Load

Slanted surface

Force

Load

High end

Low end

Slanted surface

The Screw

A **screw** is a simple machine. It consists of a pole with a sloped ridge that spirals around it. This ridge is called a **thread**.

People can use screws to hold things together. When a screw is turned, it pulls the two pieces toward each other. A jar with a twist-on lid is a type of screw. It has a thread. As you turn the lid, it is forced against the jar.

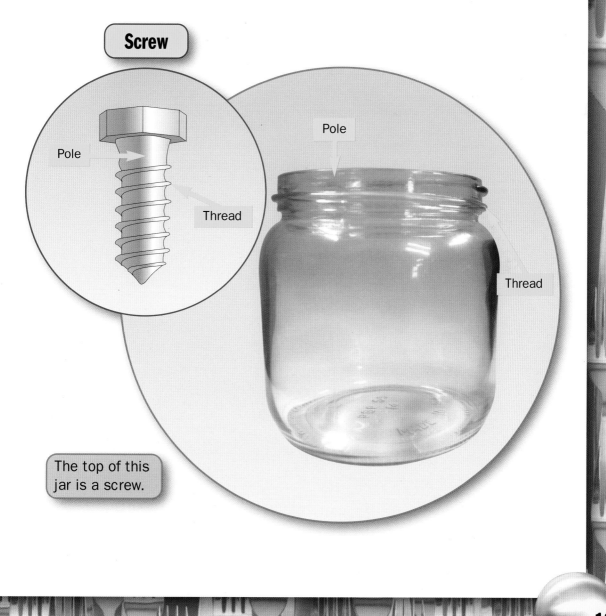

Screw

Pole

Thread

Pole

Thread

The top of this jar is a screw.

The Wheel and Axle

Another kind of simple machine is the **wheel and axle**. This machine has a wheel that is connected to a pole. The pole is called an axle. The wheel and axle always turn together. Turning the bigger wheel makes the smaller axle turn more slowly but with more force. Turning the axle makes the bigger wheel turn more quickly but with less force.

A doorknob is a type of wheel and axle. The doorknob is the wheel. The bar that is attached to the doorknob is the axle. When you turn a doorknob, you turn the axle as well. The axle moves the latch that holds the door closed.

This doorknob is a wheel and axle.

Wheel and Axle

Wheel

Movement

Axle

Force

Latch

Movement

Axle

Wheel

Force

The Pulley

A simple **pulley** is a wheel with a groove in its rim. A rope in the groove wraps around the wheel. One end of the rope is tied to a load. If you pull down on the other end, you can lift the load up.

People use pulleys to raise, lower, and move loads. Some outdoor umbrellas have pulleys. When you raise or lower these umbrellas, you use a pulley.

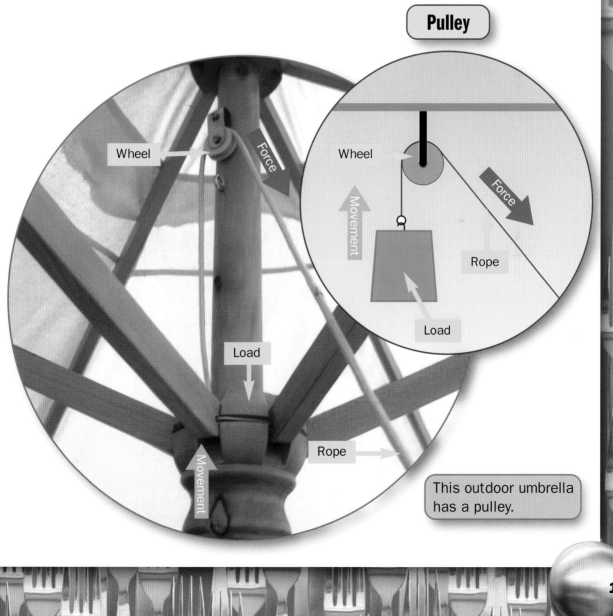

Pulley

Wheel

Force

Wheel

Movement

Force

Rope

Load

Load

Rope

Movement

This outdoor umbrella has a pulley.

Working with Machines in the Home

Most homes have both simple and **compound machines** in them. Compound machines are made up of two or more simple machines put together.

> **compound machines** 💡
> machines that are made up of more than one simple machine

Corkscrew

A corkscrew is a compound machine. It is made up of a screw and levers. It is also made up of a wheel and axle. A corkscrew helps people get corks out of bottles.

Wheel

Axle

Lever

Screw

BBQ Sauce

This corkscrew is a compound machine.

Faucet

A faucet is another compound machine. It is made up of a wheel and axle, and a screw. The faucet handle is the wheel. The axle attached to the faucet handle is also a screw. When you turn the handle one way, the screw turns. It lifts a rubber ring, called a washer. Water can then flow under the washer. Turning the handle the other way moves the washer down. This stops the flow of water.

Faucet

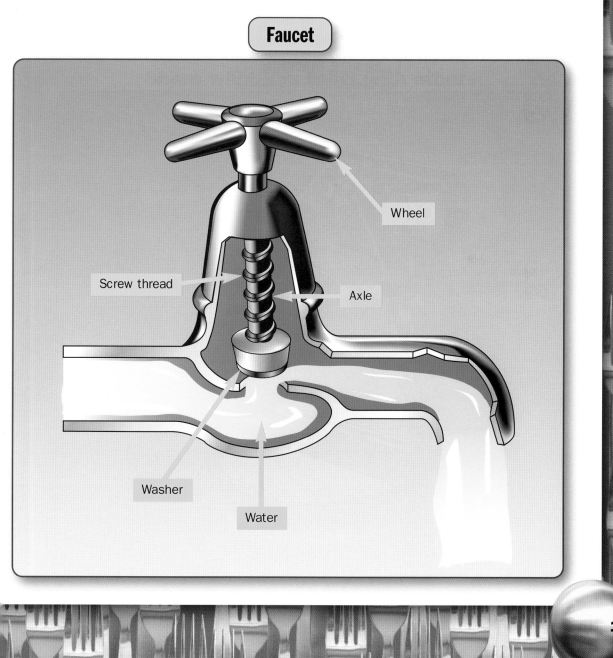

Wheel

Screw thread

Axle

Washer

Water

Labeled Photograph

Photographs show you real-life examples of ideas discussed in books or articles.

A **labeled photograph** provides extra information. The labels show you the important parts of the photograph you should be looking at.

Look back at the labeled photographs on pages 10–15. These are labeled examples of simple machines around the home. The labeled photograph on page 21 is an example of a compound machine used around the home: a can opener.

How to Read a Labeled Photograph

1. **Read the title.**
   The title tells you the subject, or what the photograph is about.

2. **Read the labels and the caption.**
   Labels and captions tell you about the subject and its parts.

3. **Study the photograph.**
   Connect the information in the photograph to what you have read in the text.

Can Opener

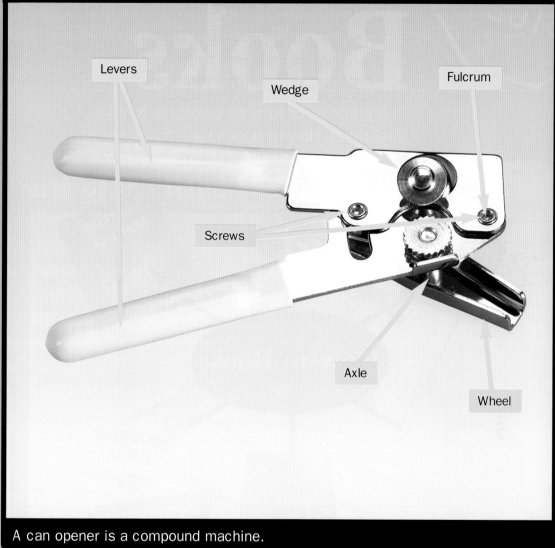

Levers

Wedge

Fulcrum

Screws

Axle

Wheel

A can opener is a compound machine.

What Can You See?

Read the photograph by following the steps on page 20. Now look back at the diagrams of compound machines on pages 17–18. Can you draw a basic diagram showing the simple machines in a can opener?

Uses for the Hand Mixer

Use the hand mixer to combine soft items, such as cake mixes or cookie dough. Do not use the hand mixer on hard items. Foods like butter and chocolate should be softened before mixing.

Safety Precautions

Take care when using the hand mixer. Follow these instructions for safe use:

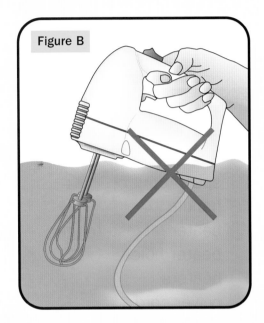

Figure B

- Watch children closely while they are using the hand mixer.

- Do not get the hand mixer or the cord wet (Figure B). If the hand mixer or the cord falls into water, unplug the cord. Do not reach into the water.

- Unplug the hand mixer when you are not using it.

- Keep hands, hair, clothing, and kitchen tools away from the beaters.

- Do not let the cord touch hot surfaces such as stove tops (Figure C). Hot surfaces may damage the cord, and the user could get an electric shock.

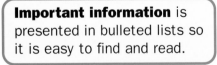

Important information is presented in bulleted lists so it is easy to find and read.

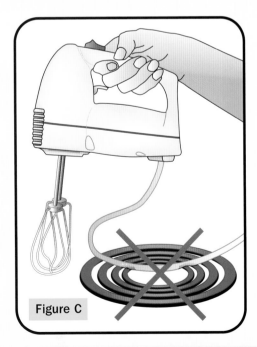

Figure C

Using the Hand Mixer

Inserting the Beaters

Before you can use your hand mixer, you need to insert the beaters.

- Make sure the hand mixer is unplugged.
- Make sure the speed control is in the OFF position (Figure D).
- Push the beaters into the beater holes until they click into place.

Running the Mixer

- Put the ingredients you want to mix into a bowl.
- Plug the hand mixer into the wall.
- Turn the hand mixer on. Use a faster speed for runnier mixtures. Use a slower speed for thicker mixtures.
- Turn the hand mixer off before you remove the beaters from the mixture.

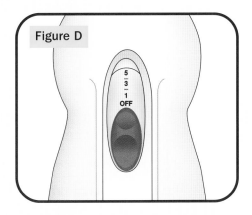

Figure D

Removing the Beaters

Remove the beaters after each use.

- Turn the hand mixer off (Figure D) and unplug it from the wall.
- Pull the beater release trigger (Figure E). The beaters will come out of the hand mixer.

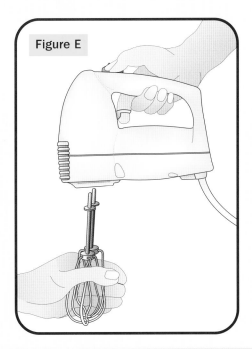

Figure E

Write
Your Own
User Manual

You have read the user manual for the hand mixer. Now you can think of a different machine that is used in the home and write a user manual for it.

1. Study the Model

Look back at the user manual on pages 23–26. What information is presented under each section? How do bulleted lists make the information easy to find and read? How do diagrams help you understand the information in the user manual?

User Manual

◆ Present the information in bulleted lists.

◆ Use diagrams to support the text.

◆ Break the information into easy-to-find sections.

◆ Include important safety precautions.

2. Choose a Machine

Think of a machine that is used in the home. Draw the design of your machine. Make notes on what job the machine does and how the machine operates. Think of any safety precautions users will need to be told about.

3. Write a User Manual

Use subheads that are similar to the ones in the hand mixer user manual to write a user manual for your machine. Present the important information clearly in bulleted lists.

4. Draw Diagrams

Draw a diagram and label the different parts of your machine. Label all the parts that you refer to in the text. Then draw smaller diagrams to help illustrate the information in your bulleted lists.

5. Read over Your Work

Read over your user manual, correcting any spelling mistakes or punctuation errors. Make sure your user manual is easy to understand. Are your instructions for use easy to follow? Have you listed all the safety precautions? Did you describe how to care for the machine? Do your diagrams clearly illustrate the text? Is there any other information the user of your machine might need to know?

Safety Precautions

- Never use the machine near water.

- Unplug the machine after use.

- Keep the machine out of reach of children.

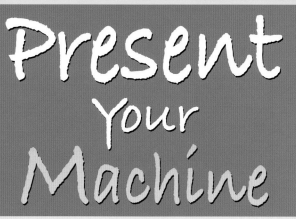

Present Your Machine

Now that you have chosen a machine and written a user manual for it, you can present the machine to the rest of the class.

How to Present Your Machine

1. Copy your labeled diagram onto an overhead transparency.

Draw the diagram clearly so you can show the different parts of your machine to the class.

2. Explain your machine to the class.

Take turns presenting your machines. Show the class the different parts of your machine on the overhead projector. Explain to the class what the machine is used for and how the machine works.

3. Explain the safety precautions.

It is important to follow the safety precautions carefully when you use any machine. Tell the class of any possible dangers with using your machine. Explain how to use the machine in the safest way possible.

4. Show the class how to care for the machine.

Tell the class how to clean, store, and care for the parts of your machine to keep it in the best working order.

Glossary

compound machines – machines that are made up of more than one simple machine

force – something that moves, changes, or stops an object

fulcrum – the fixed point on which a lever turns or swivels

inclined plane – a slanted surface that is higher at one end than the other; also called a ramp

lever – a straight bar or rod that rotates about a fixed place

load – an object that a simple machine moves, stops, or changes

machines – tools or other devices that help people do work

pulley – a grooved wheel and rope system, used to move loads

screw – a pole with a ridge called a thread that spirals around it

simple machines – devices that change how forces act

thread – a sloped ridge that wraps around the pole of a screw

wedge – an object with one or more sloping sides that may end in a sharp edge or point

wheel and axle – a wheel joined to a pole or rod

work – the result of force moving, stopping, or changing an object

Index